Little Pills of Comfort

by

Kitty Clairmont

Published by New Generation Publishing in 2014

Copyright © Kitty Clairmont 2014

First Edition

The author asserts the moral right under the Copyright, Designs and Patents Act 1988 to be identified as the author of this work.

All Rights reserved. No part of this publication may be reproduced, stored in a retrieval system or transmitted, in any form or by any means without the prior consent of the author, nor be otherwise circulated in any form of binding or cover other than that which it is published and without a similar condition being imposed on the subsequent purchaser.

www.newgeneration-publishing.com

 New Generation Publishing

Acknowledgements

Heartfelt thanks to everyone who helped me make this book possible:

Thank you to my talented son Marcus who helped me to turn a few scribbles into a manuscript with a beautiful cover.

To my friends for tirelessly proof reading and encouragement.

To my family for support and constant advice, my God given children – Marcus, Leon and Leotie who are forever my inspiration and motivation.

To Lizzie who helped me realise its potential and worth to others as well as myself, and finally but not least Agnes who also made me feel that I had a worthwhile gift and message.

To all those who believed I could do it – thank you.

Contents

1. Little Pills of Comfort (I) — p.9
2. Cuddle Time — p.11
3. Friday Love — p.12
4. Fairy Flower Wishes — p.13
5. Thank you for the Love — p.14
6. Ready for the Weekend — p.15
7. Manic Week — p.16
8. Weekend Swirl — p.17
9. Feel the Sunshine Today — p.18
10. Knitting Meditation — p.19
11. The Meeting — P.20
12. Tidy up Time! — P.21
13. Money — p.22
14. Every Success — p.23
15. You are not alone — p.24

16.	Feathers	p.25
17.	Angelic Hum	p.27
18.	Am I Beautiful?	P.28
19.	Broken Hearted	p.31
20.	On a Wing	p.33
21.	Fairy in the Coffee Pot	p.34
22.	Together we are Spirit	p.35
23.	Angelic Love	p.37
24.	Not so hard	p.38
25.	Showering you with love	p.39
26.	Somewhere over the rainbow	p.40
27.	Touch my cheek	p.41
28.	Not Over	p.42
29.	Golden Touch	p.43
30.	Crystal Health	p.45
31.	Little Pills of Comfort (II)	p.47
32.	Panic	p.48

33.	Depression	p.50
34.	Ask for what you need	p.52
35.	Living Rainbow (I)	p.54
36.	Living Rainbow (II)	p.54
37.	Help...I need somebody	p.56
38.	Hierophant	p.58
39.	Toothfairy	p.60
40.	Candlelight	p.62
41.	If you go down to the woods today	p.63
42.	Lavender Blue	p.64
43.	A Cauldron of Bubbles	p.65
44.	Leotie's Lullaby	p.67
45.	The Reality of Parenthood – a short byte	p.68
46.	Have times changed?	p.72
47.	Hand in hand	p.74
48.	Twinkle Twinkle	p.75

| 49. | Reiki | p.78 |
| 50. | Little Pills of Comfort (III) | p.79 |

Little Pills of Comfort (1)

Surrounded by used tissues
head over a steaming bowl
Paracetamol or sipping Lemsip in a bid to rid this cold

I send you a purple
pill to block
the negativity of sneezes

a green one
for recovery
from your coughing fit diseases

a yellow one
for appetite
that taste buds will again bloom

and an orange one
to give the nerve
to leave your dark sick room

a red one
to will fire your power
and help you realise

you're beautiful
despite your runny nose
and streaming eyes

with all of this I send a cup
of lavender coloured dew
collected from the flowers
the garden spirit blessed specially for you.

Cuddle Time

Feeling a little fragile
Monday morning
once again
the wind a little too cold
a damp and drizzling rain

Here's a cuddle
to warm the cockles
warm the cold tip of your nose
and fill you up with sunshine
from your eyebrows to your toes

Just remember that you carry
not just your brolly
but a love
that's given by the many
and especially from above

Friday Love

Yet another week is over
for some its flown
for others dragged

Last day of the week at your post
leaving your work
tagged in piles

As you head into the weekend
free...or are you really?
Shopping...cleaning...

Do something just for YOU...I mean
it needn't be
dull or boring

Sugar coat it, change prescription
Choose location
Or duration

Surreal or real or fantasy
Few more hours
Plan it...live it

Flower Fairy Wishes

May the flower fairies strew your path with wishes
petals soft to cushion your tread

May their scent fill your inner being with heaven
and carry you high on the clouds

Thank you For The Love

So much support it brings tears to my eyes...
more than expected, truly a
surprise...

Thank you for uplifting me with the angel wings of friendship

Thank you for helping me to focus on my task with insight and serenity

I feel so privileged, I have to swallow...
I've never felt so all embraced in
love...

Ready For the Weekend

Someone fast forwarded the week on me
where did it all go?
I had so many plans and chores to complete
now I really don't know...

On the other hand - boy! I'm sick of the slog
I need to catch a few snores
my duvet is calling and I'm gonna start crawling
back into my bed on all fours!

Manic Week

This week is a little crazy for me
are you going through this too?

Is it the rain?
or the wind that blows
such random events
that wrinkle the toes?

this is for you as well then....

may your worries be lifted
your cares blown away
feel lifted and cared for
as you sail through the day....

Weekend Swirl

As you hurry along
with bags of shopping
as you put your head down against the wind…

take in the autumn colours
feel the reds, oranges and yellows

drink them into your body
feel them fill up your soul

As you hurry along
your busy weekend
take some time to feel part of your world…

Feel The Sunshine Today

Let the sun shine through your fingers
like you did when you were small
marvel at your shadow
see that you walk tall

Feel the warmth caress your skin
breathe in each little ray
and let the sun cleanse every worry
and help you smile today....

Knitting Meditation

knit one   purl one

love   money

a yarn   of each

knit   together

interlock   stitches

lengthy   scarf

wrap   around

so   tight

snug   glee

knit   ting

need   less

in   in

terrupting   silence

The Meeting

He stepped into the room gingerly

the dog strained at the leash

his body trembled slightly forward

the dog pulled and panted

closer and closer

they met

at last

Lick!

Tidy Up Time!

Tidy up time!
Tidy up time!
teachers frantically cry
gathering children like flowers
who float away like butterflies
on a breeze
of laughter

Tidy up time!
Tidy up time!
toys are put hastily away
ready and waiting for another day
the breeze of laughter fades
back into the quiet of the classroom again.

Money

Money's too tight to mention...goes the song
too right..I nod

maybe another way to look at not having enough meat for dinner
is that I could try out a new vegetarian recipe

not having enough for new clothes
an opportunity to browse ebay and charity shops...
I do love a bargain.

Bargain hunt...lets investigate the attic
pity I don't have any valuable antiques eh?

win on the lottery?
not likely think I!

still, cuddles are free, so are kisses
at home I have plenty of those
I can have the icing at least
...if not the cake!

Every Success

Every success begins with a dream
A dandelion head of ideas
Blown out into the universe
Where sometimes the criticism and sneers

Cause it to waver and weave
Weep and wither unless
The warmth of an angel's kiss strengthens its roots
And it blooms into a success

You are not alone

Just because you didn't see it
Doesn't mean it wasn't there

Just because you didn't feel it
Doesn't mean you were not touched

Just because you didn't hear it
Doesn't mean your name wasn't called

Just because you didn't smell it
Doesn't mean it didn't waft round you

See it..feel it...hear it...smell it...how?

With your heart dear love
With your mind my sweet

Then you will
see it...hear it...smell it

And realise that you are
never alone

Feathers

I dusted, I cleaned, it was bright as a pin
I did it to drown out the noise in my brain
I was just about to polish again
When I noticed a feather right next to the bin

A feather? From where? I've no goose down or eider,
No pigeons or budgies that could moult on my floor
I squint at its details whilst I hold open the door
I'm awake, I'm not sleeping, haven't touched any cider

Lips pursed, fingers tight, I pick it up like dynamite
It feels soft and silky, I trace its length with fingertips
Amazed at the change of my mood, no longer flight or fight
I hold it up into the light

Pure white...whiter than snow
It almost gleams, it almost shines
Each tip so perfect top to tail, in perfect lines
So white there is a glow

I turn and spin, I am too slow
I could have sworn, but then again, the corner of my eyes deceived me
But look, Yes, another white angelic feather
Upon the floor right here, resting on my foot and second toe

I saw no-one
Heard nothing
But know
Everything

Angelic Hum

Listen to my inner song
my heart beats out the rhythm
my mind sings melodies that vary
can you hear them amidst the throng
of fear and worry, pain and grief?
I struggle to hear the chorus
my woes crash wave-like in a storm
that sweeps towards a reef

Raise me out of engulfing deluge
and stand me on the waves
so I can hear your homeward humming
Leading me to your refuge

where soaked to the skin, you dry off my pain
and where I am bruised, you heal my self doubts
Lead me - I'll follow - this time I won't waiver
please show me my spiritual path again

Am I Beautiful?

Pull the duvet back over my head
my hair is doing an alien impression
neither combs or grips are gonna tame this mane
look at the top! its reaching for heaven!

(Solution: a hat)

Check my skin out...I'm retreating into adolescence
bizarre because the rest of its wrinkling
you'd have thought I've done nothing but laugh all day long
for the crows have set up a fort in the crinkling!

(Solution: dark glasses)

Blame the dryer for the fact that everything feels tight
the waistband's cutting off my circulation
there's a camel toe staring me straight in the face
and that zip won't withstand any vibration

(Solution: elasticated trousers and a baggy jumper)

Meant to go to the dentist but I chickened out
and those Parl Drops were as useless as candy
it's a shame cos I'm wearing yellow today and it clashes
wonder if I've got any sandpaper handy?

(Solution: not to smile)

I pass the full length mirror and catch sight
of my reflection
An aged, overweight ninja stares right back at me
— at least I think it does
It's obviously colour blind and eaten way too many takeaways
and then in my mind I hear this buzz...

(You're beautiful)

Maybe it was that slit of sunshine that hit the mirror where I stood
or maybe my aged brain cells have at last begun to decay
but I took that hat off, changed my clothes and

beamed a great big smile
and taking my angel by the arm, we opened the door and stepped outside to face the bright new day

(Solution: if the angels think you're beautiful...then you are!)

Broken Hearted

For those who cannot fit the broken pieces of their
Heart together
For those who cannot get the sticky tape to stick
For those who thought those words meant you'd be
joined
Forever

The heart is a resilient part with restorative
powers you can't imagine
Sure it takes some time to mend the cracks and
regularly beat again
But it's stronger than you would ever believe
because it was given to us from
Heaven

We were given a heart that can show others
compassion, love and greatest of all
A mirror to see what pain they inflict as it shatters
onto the floor
For how else could the world see the anguish they
cause —
it's a massive wake up call

Of course no-one wants to be nominated a martyr,
no-one wants to be the chosen
Cure
But without suffering some people would never
evolve
As humans choosing to love
it's a pain to endure

Against hate, against poverty, abuse ...oh the list
grows day by
Day
To feel joy one must know sadness, to feel love
you've felt hate
Only love and compassion are the only things
standing in oppression's way

While your heart heals - oh loved one
know you can share
All your tears and your pain here with me
The more pain you have felt, the more you'll be
loved
Who cares? The angels in heaven and
those here on earth, your friends care.

On a Wing

Flying over to you
on a wing
on a prayer

hovering in the breeze
of the dawn
between the leaves
and the branches

to settle in a pocket of
sunshine
on a dappled docket leaf

feeling the warmth of companionship
til the wind returns for me

scoops me up
with its wing
and carries me home to bed once more

Fairy in the Coffee Pot

"There's a fairy in the coffee pot!" the little boy exclaimed,
and ran excitedly to his mum,
"Not now my darling, go and play...
"I'll look when I am done."

"But mum - she's doing the backstroke!"
he pulled her apron strings,
But mum resumed her polishing
and tidying of things.

He stared at the little fairy
she winked a cheeky wink
wide eyed he ran back to mother
who was standing by the sink -

"Mum, mum..she's got no clothes on!"
"Now Charlie, don't fib to me!"
"I clearly saw her dressed...besides...we don't have a coffee pot...
she's playing in the tea!"

Together we are Spirit

We come from the depths of the ocean
from the bones of our ancestors lost at sea;
we come from the ashes on hilltops,
timeless sufferings make up the marrow of me.

We seek out each other's spirit,
joining past and present in a herd of wild horses;
not constrained by the physical
but driven by spirit towards metaphysical.

We are the power of the ocean,
the strength of the wind that burns darkness
before us;
we are flesh of our flesh incarnate,
together we are spirit and must –

Heal each other and love one another;
where one is weak the other show strength,
share knowledge and where we have come from
for Together we are Spirit and roam the length

Of this cosmos, this universe
from whence we have come and where we'll return once more.
Run the surf with me fellow spirits -
Hail our totems...bang the drums...Spirit hear us roar!

Angelic Love

Am I an earth angel?
I have absolutely no idea
I know that I have work to do
now that I am here.

If I am an earth angel
then you must be one too
for I gain inspiration
from everything YOU do.

We knew it wouldn't be easy
that's why we send this love
to help each other in every way
get guidance from above.

Not so hard

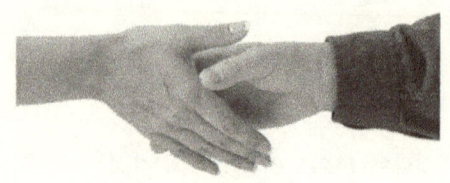

Showing love is not so hard to do
holding out a hand in love especially to you
wiping tears that furrow down
picking you up when you are down
...its not so hard to do

Showing you a mirror to show your beauty pure
giving you some comfort to help you to endure
sharing that box of chocolates
while you get over that nut
.....its not so hard to do

Remember that I'm always here to lend a helping hand
to shield you from the scorching sun and
from the drowning rain
again and again
...its not so hard to do

Showering you with love

I heard the weather forecast
they predicted "overcast and rain"
I thought of how you must have shuddered
I thought of you again...

I imagined drops of love and strength
falling softly on your head
and rainbows flying high above
overcasting protection instead

Puddles of joy like when we were young
and into the dark and gloom
so much light within and without you
for sorrow there'll be no room

So as you put your brolly up
Remember to look and see
the raindrops are pure drops of love
for you especially from me.

Somewhere over the rainbow

Somewhere over the rainbow
my troubles fly on the back of a cloud
bluebirds sprinkle blessings row upon row
upon the budding heads of the crowd.

Somewhere over the rainbow
music and songs fill the breeze
caressing soft lashes softly so
their tears are carried to the seas.

Somewhere over the rainbow
come and climb the colours with me
singing lullabies over the chimney pot tops as we go
painting sunsets and rises for all who can see.

Touch my cheek

I called your name in the deep dark night
you came into my dreams
with whispers of love you brushed the cobwebs away

We climbed grassy slopes, bathed in the golden sunlight
hand in hand, step mirroring step
I held you close and felt your love for me

All too soon the morning came
Its long fingers wrapping around you and stealing you away
my angel...my love....I know you cannot stay

Just touch my cheek before you leave
leave the imprint of your lips
on my tear streaked cheeks...before you go

Not Over

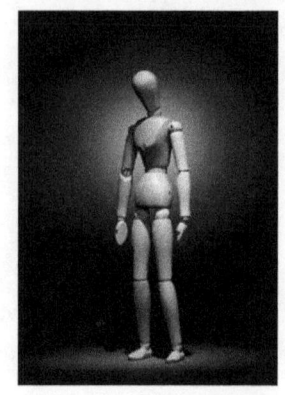

"She's not over it"

Just a little too sad
tears spring easily
even after twenty years...

Your face is reflected in theirs
They're grown men now
grown men who reflect the shape of your jaw
The crinkle of your eyes
Your smile reflected there
The face I loved...the face I still love

People don't understand
They don't realise that you're too hard to forget
Everything reminds me
Even after all these years

I'm not over it
Will never be over it
Will never be over you

Golden Touch

All they know is how to put you down
Biting, scratching insults and criticisms
My back is a raw red scab

"She's changed"

I just didn't fancy cleaning up the mess
My ears hurt
Fingernails chipped

Sympathy...?

Seeking refuge in the garden
I can't hear the phone from here
I came across white petals wind strewn on my
garden swing seat

(five...six)

I look around to find their source
No blossom trees in sight
Not left, nor right

Confusion!

Yet there they lie
Soft and fragile
Smiling at me, soothing my pain

'Heaven sent?'

Like a soothing balm on the tongue lashings on my back
Invisible angelic fingers apply the salve
A golden touch that soothes

Remind me that there is beauty in the world
Remind me that they're always there
Even when others are not

(relief)

Remind me that there is gentleness in the world
remind me that they are always there
Always there

(always there)

Crystal Health

Moonstone – woman's companion
Mother Earth stone keeping my emotions in balance
Its powdery pale blue stones reflecting a night moon
Iridescent enveloping my wrist
Calming my inner tidal waves
Embracing my inner fears and tears

Tigers Eye – to help me during my meeting
Giving me clearer perception and insight
The boldness of a tiger
Its fiery hues burning bright
Without the brutality
Just the humanity of spirit

Turquoise – my ecological friend
Enhancing my creativity
Nurturing my ability to communicate
My loyalty and friendship
Protecting me from pollutants
Seen and unseen

And a Rose Quartz at my neck
Stroking my heart
Reminding me
That I need to show myself love
That I am worthy of love
To show compassion and give forgiveness

Thus armed
I am ready to take on the day's challenges
Protected
Nurtured
Enveloped in Earth's gifts
A lovely manifestation of the Creator's love

Little Pills of Comfort (II)

What
Gives the soul
most comfort and joy?
Is it not the love received?
Eyes that wrinkle and twinkle
Lips that turn up towards the
sun. A small gracious gesture,
a door held open or a friendly
banter whilst in the queue that
has you just on the brink of
ranting. Stops you. Makes
you realise that wherever
whenever you may need
them - little pills of
comfort are
Free

Panic

How do you get to where you want to go?
(one step at a time)
When you can't move forward, frozen by fear
[fear of the unknown]
Palms sweating, pulse racing
Heart beating like a drum about to burst its seams
[fear perpetuating fear]

How do you get to where you want to go?
(one step at a time)
Breathe...listen to your breathing
Press Pause
Slow down
Reduce
Release

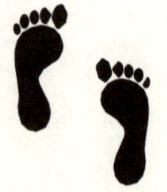

Crystal selection
You grab, you hold
Onto your sanity
And breathe the colour
Breathe the light

[feeling the power]
Flow through your veins
Gaining strength
To visualise your goals

How do you get to where you want to go?
(one step at a time)

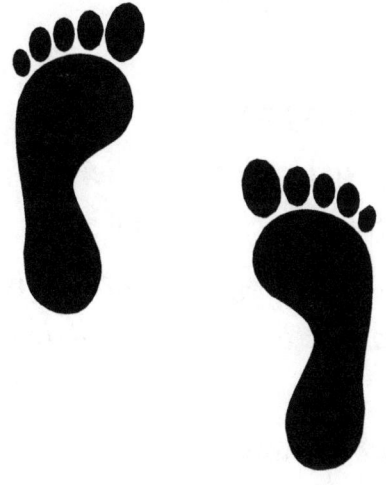

Depression

My old friend, I know you well
Like an old boyfriend who won't quite leave
Waiting for a lonely moment
A moment of weakness
Of loneliness
Of cold sheets and unwiped tears
To invite himself into my mind

Like a squatter refusing to leave
Feet up, spreading your clutter where it falls
No responsibility for the chaos you cause
You gained entrance to my muddled mind
Because I failed to put up adequate defences

'Better the devil you know'
    I don't think so

I must not travel down your rabbit warren like a demented Alice
Taking potions that only make me lose myself
Children sleeping soundly in their beds have no idea

Of how I crumble as soon as their heads hit the pillow

How I wail
Now it's safe to let loose my demon of despair

My old friend – we need to break up
I must arm myself with vitamins and minerals
Herbal supplements that enrich my brain
So addled with confusion

No shame in crying to my counsellor
No shame in voicing my fear
That there will be a knocking at my door
To take my babies away

I am strong, I am woman
I will seek the help I need
Surely it is better to accept the helping hand
To put up fences, build defences
Than to battle alone
And watch it all collapse

'Better the devil you know'
I don't think so

Ask for what you need

Give voice
To your expectations

Give voice
To what you need

Silence only breeds silence
And the hush is never ending

Give voice
To what your heart needs

Give voice
To what your arms crave

Loneliness has no company
And it never wipes the tears

Give voice
And hear the answer

Give voice
And share your dreams

Only then can wishes come true
Only then can you truly be you

Living rainbow (I)

Red and yellow
Blue and pink
Purple and orange and green

I can see a rainbow
Taste a rainbow
Feel a rainbow...can you?

Living rainbow (II)

Red seeping into orange feathery petals
A bright yellow sanctum filled with pollen for the bees

Pink and purple frettels
Majestically crowning a vibrant green stem

Fragrant flowers on my kitchen table settle
Marigold, Cornflower, Carnation and Violet
Crunchy salad leaves of the Dandelion frolic
With a seasoning of peppery Nasturtium and wild Garlic

Some herby Basil, Rosemary, lemony Thyme,
Sautéd Onion, Garlic, and Chilli Pepper to taste divine

Sweet Jasmine tea or a Dandelion root coffee
Sweetened with honeycomb courtesy of the bumble bee

I can see a rainbow
Feel a rainbow
Taste a rainbow too

Help...I need somebody

Asking for help
is not as easy as it sounds.
Not when the hounds
of debt bite at your heels and yelp
as you kick them away.

Handing someone that ball of string
that unravels all your secrets,
your guilt, your regrets.
The chaos that it may bring
is enough to scare.

When you've reaped what you've sown
When the boulder
Is too much weight to shoulder
on your own.
You need somebody.

Let them in,
help organise the mess,
straighten out what's depressed,
empty your mind's bin
and clean out your thoughts.

There's no shame
in accepting kindness or good deeds
to help you clear out the weeds.
Why carry the blame?
you're not Superman or Wonder Woman!

'No man is an island'
So John Donne tells us all, when
you can't carry the ball,
take their hand,
share the load.

Stop repressing...release
let them ease the pain
that threatens to drive you insane.
Gain some peace
Lay down your burden.

New connections and ideas
share the sorrow and wipe the tears
that have built up over the years.
Blow the cobwebs and the fears.
Ask for help...you need somebody

Hierophant

Amber eyes burning bright
Like shining stars in darkest night
Seeking searchlights to and fro
Into the forest foliage below

Spying scurrying servile prey
Burrowing into the forest affray
Swooping silently on windless wings
Lucky dipping doom stricken things

Wire sharp its claws extend
To snatch a prize that can't defend
And to its nest a silent return
Amber eyes with hunger now do burn

Exact, retract whilst beak devours
Each entrail till the dawn's wee hours
And once again its hooded lids
Close soft and sleeps as morning bids

Snowy White and Tawny Brown
In barns they slumber on feathered down

Keepers of the stories told
Hierophant and spirit old

Credited universal truths and myths
Intellectual lofty assigned gifts
Wisdom through the ages stored
And bones of mice that it has gnawed.

Tooth Fairy

Parents wonder why
Their child begins to cry
Their tooth held out in tear filled hand
'Why that tooth will fly to fairyland!'

What they do not know and can't understand
Are the fears that are conjured by the imp from this unknown land
What kind of creature from darkest abyss
Would take a child's tooth into a fairy abyss?

What craven and hungry, dark riding imp
Light as a feather, agile like a chimp
Snatches a tooth in the blink of an eye
Leaves a coin in its place, whisks it up to the sky

And what will it do with that tooth, pray do tell?
Does it lie in a tooth palace resembling hell?
White gleaming turrets and white marbled floors
Playing skittles with wee teeth that rattle the doors?

Why does she cry this wee little one?
And hide her milk tooth, for her it's not fun
Because she knows better than us I do fear
The dark fairy's kiss is a price that's too dear.

Candlelight

        S
      oft
      warm
     amber light
    radiating with
    outstretched fingers
    touching my forehead
    touching my mind
    touching my soul
      Lifts
My being whispers tO
Its flamen molten corE
Its waxy structure holD
Still time in a loving bracE
My breath makes the flamE
Dance like a heathen pagaN
But it carries my prayers oN
To God and the Angels for I
Their earth angel tire of endS
And so few beginnings thaT
Must wait until I have learneD
My lesson which is to forgivE
And love to help others abovE
All forgive and help myselF

If you go down to the woods today

Trickling brook
Tickling my fingers
Bravely I slip my toes into its soft current
Making me spasm with innocent joy and shiver
This gentle baby rhythmic river

Mossy bank
Soft beneath my limbs
Cushioning my fall from grace
In this enchanted blessed place

Leafy enclave
Boundary guarded by majestic trees
Keeping me safe and sound
Impenetrable to sound other than nature found

My safe haven both green and blue
Elements of water and earth
Quelling the fires within
Gentling soothing my intellectual din

Lavender Blue

Lavender blue looks purple to me
Lavender green the leaves you mean?
What colour would give the scent
That wafts in the breeze sent?

Soothing, relaxing a cure for most ills
A natural high for a down not illegal
Midwifery cure and infant aid which
In olden times would burn a white witch

Though they laugh when I brandish my lavender oil
For corporeal cuts and mental assoilments
I keep it close by me, a bottle or sprig piece
They never say no to the deliverer of peace

A Cauldron of Bubbles

Round about the bath we go:
In the perfumed petals throw.
Bath bomb, coloured in two-tone
Purchased with pennies of thirty-one
Bubble Bar which I have got,
You get thrown first into the charmed pot.

Double, double toil and trouble;
Banish'd to the cauldron of bubble.

Fillet of a lavender cake,
In the cauldron bubble and bake;
Eye of newt and candied frog,
Kissing lips and chocolate log,
Snacking treats- a jellied ring,
my bag of tricks I rush off to bring
For charm against our stress and trouble,
Like a heaven-broth boil and bubble.

Double, double toil and trouble;
Banish'd to the cauldron of bubble.

Bathing in the light of moon;
Punk'd hairstyles that droop too soon;
Fingers of a little girl
entwine with mother's and unfurl,-
Make the bathwater thick and bubbled:
Relieving tension and all that's troubled.
Lathering flannel, laughter, giggles
Warm wrapping arms and drying wiggles
Finger painted scented face
Add thereto a childhood smudgeon,
For ingredients of our bubble cauldron.

Double, double toil and trouble;
Banish'd to the cauldron of bubble.

Cool it to our perfect mood,
Then the charm is firm and good.

Leotie's Lullaby

Lavender's Blue diddle diddle
Lavender's Green
When I am King diddle diddle
You shall be Queen

When the moon's high diddle diddle
When the moon's bright
I will love you diddle diddle
With all of my might

...Goodnight

The Reality of Parenthood – a short byte

[Relating and swapping stories during a mother's tea circle which resembles a comedy night at Jongleurs]

"I played a psychic detective today,
damage on the walls with crayon...they wouldn't say;
falling skies of feathers from a dilapidated pillow,
kids renacting 'The Fugitive', I don't know."

"To tell you the truth I have my own version of Keeping up with the K...ids, but in my house it takes on a new meaning"

"I applied all my skills in forensic investigation to examine rivers of possibilities,
Emulating Poirot but feeling more like Miss Marple in the midst of hostilities.

I interrogated the usual suspects: **Mad Max** [who enjoys jumping on everything especially on our poor unsuspecting cat Zig Zag who has to live up to her name in order to survive]

Bert the conqueror [known for his Houdini like qualities and surprise attacks on his brother and sister and on occasion me, when I attempt a sleep in]

And Nigella who bites [an embarrassing trait especially in the park playground where inevitably within five minutes of her arrival, at least three children will be screaming their heads off and parents warn their unsuspecting children "Becareful of her, Nigella bites!]"

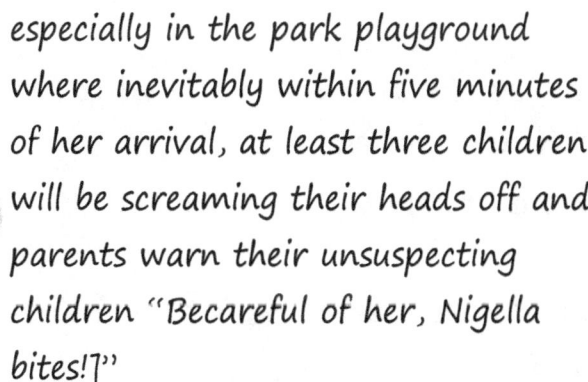

"What was apparent and elementary was your inability to quell the fights! Lol"

"Very droll –"

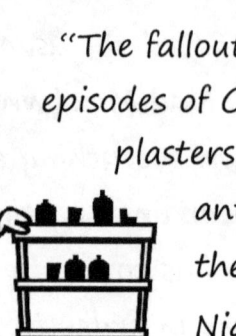
"The fallout inevitably resembles episodes of Casualty, armed with plasters, disinfectant and antiseptic cream, I tend to the wounded,
Night times see me tackling the great Unsolved Mysteries and Searching for Big Foot under the bed — never satisfactorily concluded.

In truth I feel like a broken old doll;
I am the ultimate Desperate Housewife who's hit a wall.
My angels threaten to dissolve what little granules of patience I possess,
I am out of depth, I must confess.

It would have been easier if their father was still around —
His accomplishments really had no bound.
A blend of American Dad and Family Guy glued to his beverage
who would astonish Cheaters - not a conducive element to parenting or marriage.

So I rise from the ashes with THAT LOOK on my face –
That sounds so familiar that my motley crew all race
to quieten down and started elbowing each other in silence,
it's taken "Mum's lost it now" to form this alliance.

We stage our version of 'Little House On The Prairie':
    choruses of "Stop it!" and "Go to sleep!" until they are weary;
    until everyone lies sleeping in a cloud of baby powder,
    and the cat finally emerges purring much louder.

"Who do you think you are?"

"I tame the untameable, the Raiders on my last nerve,
Will I never get the recognition I deserve?
I am a Mother – I am a woman of valour
I do the best that I can – Masha Allah."

Have times changed?

Like Romeo and Juliet
our families disagree,
they cannot reconcile or bless
the love twixt you and me.

You're Black – I'm White,
I'm dark – you're fair,
The wrong religion,
they do not care.

They cannot see that in your eyes
reflected there is God;
they think that you are just too old
– they just think that you are odd.

Too strange to look beyond the shell –
Too weird, what would they think?
No matter that it breaks my heart
and drives me to the brink...

It cannot be –
and yet...it can;
For God is in us all.

My prayers I'll send in multitude
and God will hear my call.

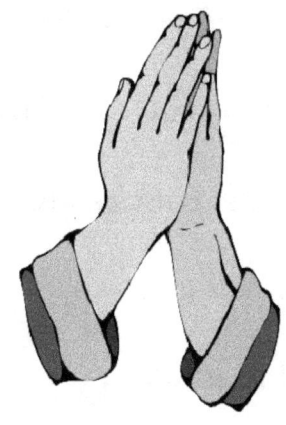

Hand in hand

Hands touching hands,

Fingers weaving through fingers;

All shades forming a network of kindred souls

empowering a change in the world.

Knock the knife out of an embittered hand,

break the fast with friends and family.

Ramadan, Christmas, Solstice and Diwali:

memories of light and love –

reflections of God in us all.

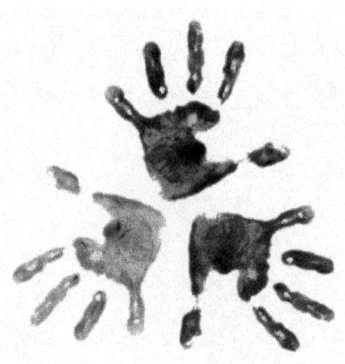

Twinkle Twinkle

I met a homeless man
who slept underneath the stars;
He seemed to be invisible
to all the people in their cars.

His chalky pictures on the floor
just brightened up my day,
even when the rain did pour
I ventured out my way –

To pop into the café and
buy a tea and cake
I'd chat to him about his life,
a picnic we would make.

He'd been a ballet dancer
on stage and seen the world;
He showed me magic stars and glitz
in stories he unfurled.

Nige was old and grey now –
his face scored deep with lines,
his limbs though long bore the stooping
that somehow age assigns.

His feet were arthritic
and pained him when it rained,
but he never regretted the profession,
his dream he never blamed.

One day I did not see him —
Nor the next, nor after that —
I learned that he had passed away —
Soon after, our last chat.

His spot beside the café
Was empty, no one there,
No brightly coloured drawings,
No stories left to share.

I missed my friend, the homeless man,
I felt a pang of pain,
For he'd become my friend you see
And I'd not see him again.

Then I looked into the night sky
such wondrous winter stars,
unnoticed by so many
as they hurried past in cars.

One twinkling **star** it caught my eye,
it even seemed to say:
"Don't cry for me! I'm dancing free!"
A tear – I wiped away.

So every time I pass his spot
I send a little prayer
To bless his soul that just might be
That twinkling **star** up there.

Reiki

Light funnelling gently
into my body,
travelling to each nerve ending
...each muscle,
easing the spasms of pain.

Funnelling into my mind
enveloping with golden hands,
my aching thoughts
and throbbing temples with gentle breath.

Touch without touch –
Healing my troubled soul
Healing my troubled heart.

I smile...
Contented, comforted;

Burden lifted...I am ready to start anew.

Little Pills of Comfort (III)

These little pills of comfort
May they bring to you
The knowledge that you're not alone
In anything you do.

You're not alone in crying
You're not alone at all
We all fall from grace at one time
We all slide down that wall

Of injustice, depression, persecution
Of bullies, death and pain
What you need is a hand to recover
That will help you stand again

We all get down on our luck
Some spiral, others soar
Be the good Samaritan, I beg you
And open up your door

Show the goodness that God gave you
Compassion to fellow man
Love each other through the agony
Turn 'can't' into 'I can'.

www.ingramcontent.com/pod-product-compliance
Lightning Source LLC
LaVergne TN
LVHW041635070426
835507LV00008B/634